SMOKE

I0139863

Vickie Ramirez

BROADWAY PLAY PUBLISHING INC
New York
www.broadwayplaypublishing.com
info@broadwayplaypublishing.com

SMOKE
© Copyright 2023 Vickie Ramirez

Cover image by Jesse Primeau

First edition: May 2023
I S B N: 978-0-88145-984-5

Book design: Marie Donovan
Page make-up: Adobe InDesign
Typeface: Palatino

SMOKE was first produced by Mixed Phoenix Theatre Group (Danielle Soames, Artistic Director) at The Studio Theatre at The Pershing Square Signature Center, New York, running from 5-21 April 2013. The cast and creative contributors were:

CONNIE FARMER.. Tanis Parenteau
ARTHUR FARMER SR...James Fall
ART FARMER JR..Matt Langer
GARY SMOKE... Brandon Oakes
KAREN SMOKE ....Sera-Lys McArthur
WOMAN/MRS SMOKE.....................................Soni Moreno
FLINT.. Alex Jacob Wilson
BREWSTER WHITE ....Raul Castillo

Director.. Richard C Aven
Scenic design...Sarah Martin
Lighting design ....Amanda Clegg Lyon
Costume design...Lux Haac
Sound design...Jeremy S Bloom
Production Stage Manager .... Liz Elise Richards

SPECIAL THANKS

To the American Indian Community House, Amerinda, The Public Theater, Steve Elm, Jim Cyrus, and Chukalokoli Native Theater Ensemble.

CHARACTERS & SETTING

CONNIE FARMER, 30, *Tuscarora, Christian, single, works at local council house.*

ARTHUR FARMER SR, 57, *Tuscarora, traditional Haudenosaunee,* CONNIE's *father.*

ART FARMER JR, 24, *Tuscarora, Christian, Army Vet, just back from Iraq.*

GARY SMOKE, 32, *Mohawk, traditional Haudenosaunee, Clan Chief, businessman.*

KAREN SMOKE, 30, *Mohawk, traditional Haudenosaunee, former beauty queen, twice divorced.*

WOMAN/MRS SMOKE, *ageless, Mohawk, traditional Haudenosaunee, when personifying* MRS SMOKE. *She is part of the spirit realm; becomes* MRS SMOKE *when she steps into the play.*

FLINT, 8-12, *otherworldly, can be played by child or adult imitating child. Twin brother of The Creator. Entirely in the spirit realm but he can actively affect the characters.*

BREWSTER WHITE, 32, *traditional Haudenosaunee, mixed-blood Mohawk, a great fondness for Jack Daniels.*

A Haudenosaunee (Iroquois) reservation in Upstate New York.

A small city nearby. The Present.

ACT ONE

Scene 1

(A Haudenosaunee Reservation in upstate New York. The recent past. Stage right, there is a sofa, a coffee table and a TV [CONNIE's apartment], stage left, there is a table, chairs and a counter [the bar]. Upstage center, there is a painting of a long wooden building, deep in the woods. This is the Longhouse. Downstage center is the "river".)

(Tableau)

(Lights up on CONNIE FARMER *[30] Tuscarora, and her father,* ARTHUR FARMER SR *[57] Tuscarora, at* CONNIE's *home, watching TV. She smokes.* BREWSTER WHITE *[32] mixed-blood, Mohawk, paces behind the sofa.)*

*(*GARY SMOKE *[32] Mohawk, having a working lunch at the bar.)*

(Downstage center, KAREN SMOKE *[30] Mohawk, beautiful—waits by the river.)*

(A young soldier enters, dressed in enlisted army fatigues. This is ART FARMER JR. *[24] Tuscarora.* KAREN *spots him as he enters and runs to him. They are obviously in love.)*

(As they embrace, a boy [8-12] in a traditional outfit dashes out from behind the Longhouse. He is invisible to all the other actors onstage as he knocks GARY's *food from his hands and mocks the lovers. This is* FLINT/TAWISKARON. *He flops down beside* CONNIE *on the sofa and messes with her, plays with her hair, steals her cigarette, etc. as the other*

actors exit. A WOMAN *[50] enters, chasing after* FLINT. *She is dressed in contemporary and traditional clothes, including a beaded buckskin bag. The decoration on the bag is basic, four rows of beading, alternating white—purple, white-purple. This is a copy of the two-row wampum.)*

(FLINT *tries to distract her, but she ignores him and pulls out a small wooden bowl. She takes out a bag of tobacco and starts an offering. He snatches away the bag and mimes pinching the tobacco and "chawing.")*

WOMAN: Tawiskaron! That's sacred tobacco!

(FLINT *shrugs. The* WOMAN *turns to the audience.)*

WOMAN: A handful 'en he? All he wants is a little attention. It's hard for him, you know? He's important—just as important as his brother. Of course that's the kid that gets all the attention— "The Creator" —okay with that title of course he does… but Tawiskaron—you can call him Flint, too…well, his gifts are a little different.

(FLINT *blows a raspberry.)*

WOMAN: Hey, now! Behave! THE MISCHIEVOUS ONE, that's another name. Some folks even call him EVIL. I don't like that word. Don't believe it was ever our word. Came with the Invaders. What they call Evil, we call confusion, displacement and despair. BAD MIND. That's what they mean when they call him Evil. BAD MIND, is another one of his names. The other one—The Creator…GOOD MIND—well sure, he's celebrated. He gave us fresh crops, green grass, sunny blue skies…roses—gotta admit, I like the roses. Flint— gave us thorns. You need thorns—or so he tells me—

(FLINT *winks.)*

WOMAN: —otherwise people might get too greedy. The Creator made flowing rivers full of tasty fish, Flint made rapids—so you can go fast…so he says—

(FLINT *mimes a canoe crashing.*)

WOMAN: Yeah. Um… Fast.

(FLINT *makes a snaking gesture with his hand.*)

WOMAN: He also made snakes. Need those too—to handle those pests out in the fields that Flint…also made—

(FLINT *makes a sucking noise.*)

WOMAN: And leeches—'kay, I'm sure there's a reason for those—

(*Encouraged,* FLINT *taps the* WOMAN *on her shoulder. She turns to face him and he makes a monstrous face.*)

WOMAN: That's not helpful. (*Beat*) Well, what do you expect? Darkness is his realm. Do we wonder why he's a handful?
They're twins and his brother gets all the attention. He isn't evil. Just stubborn. Here's another one. Stubborn too.

(*The* WOMAN *points toward* CONNIE. FLINT *dangles the tobacco in front of her, luring her to the river as she tries to snatch it from his hands.* FLINT *dodges her a few times, finally letting the tobacco drop on the ground. As* CONNIE *crouches before it the* WOMAN *steps up to her. She strokes one hand on* CONNIE'*s hair.*)

CONNIE: (*Little Connie voice*) I don't understand, Mama, why can't I go to the Longhouse with Brewster?

WOMAN: (*As* CONNIE'*s mother*) Longhouse is for the True-Indians. The Ongwehoneweh—Mama's Christian. We can't go.

CONNIE: But I'm Indian too! I wanna go with Brewster!

WOMAN: (*As* CONNIE'*s mother*) Sweetie you're not Longhouse. You can't. Mama's different. Because you're a little bit of me too, you're different. Some things just aren't open to us.

CONNIE: That's not fair!

(The WOMAN *snaps her fingers and* CONNIE *freezes.)*

WOMAN: *(To audience)* Can't get over it, this one. Never could accept some things can't change for wishing.

(The WOMAN *strolls over and taps* FLINT *on the shoulder. Stubborn to the end he shakes his head.)*

(The WOMAN *waits, then grabs him by the ear dragging him offstage. As they leave,* CONNIE *snaps out of it.)*

CONNIE: Hello?

(Adult CONNIE *finds the tobacco pouch. She picks it up gently not noticing as* BREWSTER *enters.)*

BREWSTER: Hey Connie!

CONNIE: Geez! Following me, again, huh?

BREWSTER: You should be so lucky. Just wanted to ask if you'd do me a favor.

CONNIE: Why am I not surprised? What do you need Brews?

BREWSTER: Hey, what's that?

CONNIE: Nothing—

*(*BREWSTER *tries to peek around* CONNIE'*s shoulder. She dodges him.)*

BREWSTER: C'mon—why you hiding it?

CONNIE: Don't know what you're talking about.

BREWSTER: Constance Marie Farmer, you're a bad liar—

CONNIE: Takes one to know one—

BREWSTER: Don't be such a chicken, tell me—

CONNIE: It's nothing— *(She shifts and the tobacco pouch drops to the ground.)*

BREWSTER: *(Picks it up)* What is that? Sacred tobacco?

CONNIE: What? I'm not allowed because I'm not Longhouse?

BREWSTER: Well, technically no but I don't care. How'd you get it?

CONNIE: I do have friends, you know.

BREWSTER: Not Longhouse ones. Except for me, of course.

CONNIE: Since when do you count as Longhouse?

BREWSTER: Oh I'm still Longhouse, not welcome there, but still am.

(BREWSTER *pulls out his a flask of bourbon and takes a nice long sip.* CONNIE *snatches back the pouch.*)

CONNIE: Don't! Not around the tobacco!

BREWSTER: Screw the tobacco, I'm thirsty.

CONNIE: Stop it, Brews, come on!

(CONNIE *pushes away the flask.*)

BREWSTER: Okay, okay, calm down. I can still show you how to do an offering, if you want?

CONNIE: What? No. It should go back to the right person.

BREWSTER: You sure? This is a one-time offer from a genuine sorta—Longhouse—

CONNIE: No thanks. I'm putting it back where I found it. (*She turns and puts on the ground.*)

BREWSTER: On the ground.

CONNIE: On the Mother.

BREWSTER: Right. Okay. So, Con…

CONNIE: What do you need Brews?

BREWSTER: Maybe I just need to see your pretty smile.

CONNIE: Huh, right—you've got your begging voice on.

BREWSTER: Woman, if you ever listened to my begging voice—

CONNIE: *(Cuts him off)* What do you need, Brews?

BREWSTER: Iron my jacket for me?

CONNIE: Oh for—seriously? First of all you guys ditch me on Art's first night home and now you want me to help you get ready?

BREWSTER: Come on, Con—you don't want me to embarrass Art—he's wearing his fancy uniform.

CONNIE: Great, he said Hi for all of five minutes and now he's heading out for some big celebration without any of the family.

BREWSTER: I'm going.

CONNIE: You don't count—

BREWSTER: Ouch!

CONNIE: I didn't mean it like that—but, he hasn't seen us for years and what's the first thing he wants to do? Party with his buddies.

BREWSTER: He needs to cut loose, Con—that's all.

CONNIE: And big sister is cordially not welcome.

BREWSTER: I didn't realize you wanted to hang with me so badly—

CONNIE: Hah! Not quite.

BREWSTER: You know the real reason the Indian population is shrinking? You're all the cruellest women alive.

CONNIE: Well it's a good thing you're going to the city, then—I hear the girls there are real sweet—

BREWSTER: Yeah, sweet sounds good.

CONNIE: Bet they'd all love a chance to spoil a handsome Indian guy—

BREWSTER: That's right—hey, did you say "handsome?"

CONNIE: *(Cuts him off)* —but try "iron my jacket" on one of them. See how well that goes over. You know how to do laundry.

BREWSTER: Yeah—but I really don't wanna.

CONNIE: Since I know you you're fine wearing a jacket that has been balled up in a bag at the bottom of your closet—I will do it.

BREWSTER: See—you love me—you know you do.

CONNIE: This is a one time offer, Brews. And I would appreciate it if you could do me a favor.

BREWSTER: Always. Never have to ask.

CONNIE: *(Beat)* Keep an eye on him tonight.

BREWSTER: He's okay. He's not the same dumb kid he was when he left, but he's okay. *(Beat)* Still thinking of leaving?

CONNIE: Past time, ennit?

BREWSTER: Better buy a comfy sofa.

CONNIE: What?

BREWSTER: First law of Native physics; cool apartment in expensive city equals Indians on my sofa.

CONNIE: Oh yeah?

BREWSTER: Better stock up the fridge, too. I'll have no money left for food after spending it all on gas.

CONNIE: Better gas than booze!

BREWSTER: More abuse! Geez Woman—

CONNIE: Poor baby. *(She exits.)*

BREWSTER: Cruellest women alive.

(End of scene)

Scene 2

(Lights the bar. ART stands at parade rest, a soda in front of him. He is wearing an enlisted army dress uniform.)

(FLINT dashes in from stage left. He's got the WOMAN's beaded buckskin bag.)

(He races toward stage right, dangling the bag like a lure. The WOMAN runs in. She and FLINT face-off. She gives him the hairy eyeball.)

WOMAN: Flint, give me the bag.

(FLINT shakes his head.)

WOMAN: C'mon. You should be more respectful of that! Do you know what those beads mean?

(FLINT pets the beads "pretty". The WOMAN grabs the bag.)

WOMAN: It's a copy of the Two-Row Wampum. Our first treaty.

(FLINT rolls his eyes/makes a face.)

WOMAN: Okay, okay—I know—silly us.

(FLINT shrugs and wanders over to poke at ART, who doesn't acknowledge him. The WOMAN gestures for him and he follows her offstage, passing KAREN, a beautiful Mohawk woman, as she enters. She spots ART and walks over, gently brushing his sleeve, but he whips around anyway—startled.)

KAREN: Hey, it's okay. It's just me.

ART: Hey—what are you doing here?

KAREN: *(Gives him a kiss)* Sorry if I startled you. I just wanted see how you're doing.

ART: Worrying about me?

KAREN: No—just wanted to say, "Hi" that's all.

ART: I'm not that fucked up 'kay?

KAREN: I know—

ART: I can handle the city and I can handle your brother.

KAREN: I know. He won't be a problem.

ART: I just wanna explain, what happened. So he knows—

KAREN: He knows you're no coward.

(Beat)

ART: He knows more than me, then.

KAREN: You were honorably discharged. They wouldn't have done that if it was your fault.

ART: It's still on my record. And your brother is—well, nothing ever goes wrong for the next big Clan Chief of the Mohawk Nation—

KAREN: That's not you talking—that's Connie. You don't know Gary and he doesn't know you. That's why you're here, right?

ART: Right. But if he says no—

KAREN: He doesn't get to. I choose my own husband. Besides, Mom likes you. She's Clan Mother. She approves he has to.

(BREWSTER enters, wearing "tie" T-shirt, and jeans and a well-pressed, but awkward fitting suit jacket.)

BREWSTER: Well, this is a fancy bar, alright— everybody's got ties!

KAREN: You invited Brewster?!

ART: No. Brews, what are you doing here?

BREWSTER: Hey. Art knows I need no invitation!

KAREN: *(To ART)* You sure you want him here? He and Gary—

ART: It's Brews.

(Beat. KAREN *accepts this.)*

KAREN: Brewster. What an unexpected surprise.

BREWSTER: Nice to see you too, Princess, we all partying together?

KAREN: No. I don't drink—remember?

BREWSTER: That's what's nice about getting my ass kicked out of the Longhouse—I don't have to remember the rules anymore.

KAREN: Well, you enjoy yourself—

BREWSTER: I will…and don't worry about our boy here—I'll make sure that he does too.

(Beat. KAREN *turns to* ART, *deliberately ignoring* BREWSTER.)

KAREN: Don't worry. It's all gonna be good.

ART: I know. I've got you, don't I?

*(*ART *and* KAREN *embrace.* BREWSTER *runs over and layers on, turning it into a group hug.)*

BREWSTER: I'm just full of the love of the world right now, aren't you guys?

(Beat)

KAREN: *(To* ART*)* Keep him on a leash, okay?

(That triggers barking from BREWSTER.*)*

ART: He won't be a problem.

(They kiss goodbye and she exits. ART *gives* BREWSTER *a death glare.)*

BREWSTER: What?

(End of scene)

Scene 3

(*Interior,* CONNIE'*s living room. It's small and contemporary, the only decorations are the bead-work and a huge quilt hanging on the wall. To the far right is a small open kitchen area, with a counter and stools.*)

(CONNIE *is in the kitchen with* ARTHUR SR. *[49]. She supervises as he prepares a Catfish.*)

CONNIE: Ick, Dad! What a big hairy ugly fish!

ARTHUR SR: Your Mother used to say that the whiskers is what makes it taste so good.

CONNIE: And you bought it, huh?

ARTHUR SR: Wasn't worth losing my dinner to argue—so I didn't.

CONNIE: Note to self, keep their food if they give you any guff.

ARTHUR SR: You're your mother's daughter, alright.

CONNIE: I'll take that as a compliment.

ARTHUR SR: You should. Your mother didn't stand for nonsense, from anyone. Just one of her gifts.

CONNIE: She could tell great stories, too.

ARTHUR SR: Yep. You get your cooking from her. Best pies on the Rez.

CONNIE: I remember watching her cook. Indian cookies, mainly.

ARTHUR SR: That's because you were always eating them as she cooked them. What do they call that? Sense memory? Easy to remember when you can still taste 'em.

CONNIE: That's her recipe I use—ennit?

ARTHUR SR: Yep. You've got her smile too. And her stubbornness. She always knew when you kids were upset. Had a sixth sense about it.

CONNIE: Okay, here we go, I knew something was coming.

ARTHUR SR: *(Beat)* You gonna run away and join the army too?

CONNIE: Nope. Ugly outfits.

ARTHUR SR: What's wrong with you, then?

CONNIE: Nothing. Nothing's wrong.

ARTHUR SR: You're not happy. I can see it.

CONNIE: I don't know. Art's back and nothing's changed. I'm still in the same house, same job—

ARTHUR SR: You're gonna leave then?

CONNIE: I don't know. I gotta figure out something. Should I stick it out in the council house in the same job for twenty years? If I'm not careful, I'm gonna become the reservation cat-lady!

ARTHUR SR: Not if Brewster has anything to say about it.

CONNIE: Oh sure, me and Brewster! I'm barely tolerated, and Brews is the only man to ever get booted from his Longhouse!

ARTHUR SR: A perfect match!

CONNIE: Dad.

ARTHUR SR: I could use some grandkids.

CONNIE: Not this again.

ARTHUR SR: Well, why not? It's been long enough.

CONNIE: Yeah? Says who?

ARTHUR SR: Children are a wonderful gift from the Creator.

CONNIE: Some people are not supposed to have kids. *(She turns away.)* What did you call that, again?

ARTHUR SR: Catfish Etouffee! I saw it on Emeril.

CONNIE: Its supposed to be Crawfish.

ARTHUR SR: What's the difference? Both of 'em have whiskers.

(End of scene)

Scene 4

*(*ART *still waits at the bar.* BREWSTER *rejoins him as* FLINT *plays bartender.)*

BREWSTER: They got TV in the john here! Now that's practical. *(He picks up the beer, drains it. Waves the empty)* Hey, what about some service?! We got a veteran here!

ART: Cut it out, Brews!

BREWSTER: If you're going to wear that thing, we might as well get some mileage out of it.

ART: C'mon man, that's not cool.

BREWSTER: Sure it is. One of the perks. You came back in one piece—you get decent service. That's how it goes. In fact, if some folks were nice, they'd buy us a drink because, you're due one.

ART: You're not.

BREWSTER: Right. Because I didn't volunteer to be bullet magnet for the government. Some folks might think I deserve a drink for wisdom.

ART: Gary will be here any minute.

BREWSTER: Fuck Gary.

ART: He's Karen's brother—and he's gonna be Clan Chief.

BREWSTER: Like I said, fuck Gary. How many people did you kill, Kid? Do you even know?

ART: Fuck you, Brews—

BREWSTER: It's just you and me right now. I gotta know. Was it worth it? The Longhouse all think you're a hero but you're all fucked-up and you have blood on your hands.

ART: So you're a pacifist, now?

BREWSTER: Hell no—I could handle it. If someone was threatening me or Connie—or you or your Dad—but it was never supposed to be you. You're the baby.

ART: A warrior's supposed to protect the people and the places he cares about. That's what I was doing.

BREWSTER: You were being used.

ART: No. I was being useful. I wasn't sitting around here everyday working a dead end shitty job, watching my life disappear while other guys my age needed me and needed my back-up. It wasn't about the big picture—it was about the one-on-one.

(Neither BREWSTER *nor* ART *notice as* GARY *[32] strolls in. Polished and professional, he is the essence of the upwardly mobile Indian.)*

BREWSTER: You were needed here, too. Your family needed you.

GARY: —You're wasting your time, Art. Brewster is not someone who understands social responsibility.

BREWSTER: Ding-Dong, Asshole calling!

ART: Brewster, please don't mess this up for me.

BREWSTER: Right. I'm a bad host. *(Turns to the bartender)* Hey, we need shots! Shots for the brave war veteran and our future Clan Chief!

*(*ART *waves away the bartender.)*

GARY: You know, they serve food here too Brews.

BREWSTER: Naw, eating makes me less thirsty.

ART: Why don't we get a table, I think a table would be good.

GARY: Sure, lets get a table. I'll get another round of drinks.

BREWSTER: *(Stares at* GARY's *suit)* He looks like an undertaker.

GARY: Nice tie. *(Ordering)* Another soda Art? And some random beer for Brewster. I'm sure it won't make a difference which one.

BREWSTER: Hey, Mr Smug Longhouse!

GARY: Haudenosaunee, Brewster, —you know better.

BREWSTER: Art just got back. He might want a beer too. Some people would say he deserves one.

ART: I'm good with the soda.

GARY: *(To* BREWSTER*)* I know it's been years since you've been to Longhouse, Brews, but even you should remember—Haudenosaunee don't drink.

BREWSTER: Well, we all know Art ain't Haudenosaunee, don't we? Not with a Christian for a Mom.

ART: I'm good with the soda.

GARY: Well, if he's marrying my sister, he's gonna respect traditional ways.

(Beat)

BREWSTER: Wait a minute—what?

ART: I would've told you, but you were too busy giving me the "War is Wrong" speech.

BREWSTER: Okay, I know you had a crush when you were a kid, but come on! She's been married twice already.

GARY: What are you saying?

ART: What does that have to do with anything?

BREWSTER: She's been around a bit.

GARY: You know, you should watch your mouth.

BREWSTER: C'mon, Art. Think about it. You just got back, you haven't even started your life, yet.

ART: It started the day I shipped out.

BREWSTER: Yeah, you saw a lot of shit over there, but—don't grab onto the first female that walks past just to feel normal.

GARY: You don't know when to quit, do you?

(GARY *steps up to confront* BREWSTER, *but* ART *intervenes.*)

ART: Hey! Stop it! Brewster, I love her. Please respect that, and respect her.

BREWSTER: This is too fast. You just got back.

GARY: This is how you support your friend? Hate to see what you'd do with an enemy.

BREWSTER: You wanna find out, keep talking.

ART: Look, I know her—okay? She wrote me every week.

BREWSTER: I think she started that with her kids as a school project.

ART: Dammit—

BREWSTER: What about Connie, Art?

GARY: What does she have to do with anything?

BREWSTER: You always said they "polluted the reservation". So why are you letting Art marry your little sister?

GARY: Art and Karen want to start with a clean slate. I'm gonna too.

BREWSTER: It's not gonna happen. *(To* ART*)* Have you told Connie?

GARY: Here we go again.

ART: Leave her out of this.

BREWSTER: This is the fuck that knocked her up and wouldn't marry her.

GARY: Art's not marrying me.

ART: Lets all calm down and sit at the table.

BREWSTER: You smug asshole.

GARY: She "lost" the baby the moment I turned her down, didn't she? Pretty convenient.

ART: Hey!

BREWSTER: She didn't make it up!

GARY: So she got rid of the baby out of spite?

ART: Wait a minute!

BREWSTER: Fuck you!

GARY: Yeah, she did. Still jealous?

Brewster snaps and swings, just as Gary swings too. Art steps between them and gets clipped by both punches.

ART: Ow, dammit.

(End of scene)

Scene 5

*(*CONNIE'*s apartment.* CONNIE *and* ARTHUR SR *watch TV.)*

ARTHUR SR: What's this we're watching?

CONNIE: It's a fashion show.

ARTHUR SR: They're just marching around in stupid clothes, where's the show in that? Is that a boy or a girl?

CONNIE: C'mon Dad.

ARTHUR SR: No, really. You can't tell these days. No man is supposed to wear those pants. One tug, they'd fall right down. Is that why you want to go to the city. Easy access?

CONNIE: *(Laughs)* Stop it!

ARTHUR SR: Maybe I need to get a pair of those pants. Wilma Longboat's looking good and Bingo night's on Thursday.

CONNIE: TMI! Please stop NOW.

(Suddenly there's a loud knocking ARTHUR SR *moves to answer it, but* CONNIE *shakes her head. Beat.* BREWSTER *enters.)*

CONNIE: Uh-Oh. Bad Night?

ARTHUR SR: Since you're in, Brewster, you should have a seat.

BREWSTER: If you don't mind, Sir, I'd like to talk to Connie.

ARTHUR SR: I'd say you're doing that right now.

BREWSTER: Alone, please.

CONNIE: Ooooh, sounds like trouble!

ARTHUR SR: Alone! Hmmmph! C'mere here boy.

*(*BREWSTER *crosses over to* ARTHUR SR ARTHUR SR *stares at him intently—then tugs hard on his pants as* CONNIE *shrieks with laughter.)*

CONNIE: You're terrible.

ARTHUR SR: Just checking. I'll head off. You two have your discussion.

(ARTHUR SR *exits.* CONNIE *strolls back over to the sofa.* BREWSTER *is still hovering.*)

CONNIE: Do you want a drink or something, Brews? I have strawberry tea.

BREWSTER: No, I'm good.

CONNIE: Well, sit down before you fall down, then.

BREWSTER: Did you know Art has been seeing Karen Smoke?

CONNIE: How is that possible?

BREWSTER: They've been writing—

CONNIE: Well, okay. Art knows what he's getting into—hah! I bet Gary is in a RAGE—

BREWSTER: Connie—

CONNIE: (*Grabs her phone*) Bad enough we're still here "polluting the rez" I can't imagine what he must think of his sister dating one of us. I think I need to give him a call!

BREWSTER: Connie—they're getting married.

(*Beat*)

CONNIE: What? You said they were penpals—

BREWSTER: It's a little more than that.

CONNIE: That's crazy—it's…well Gary will never allow it.

BREWSTER: He was there tonight.

(*Beat*)

CONNIE: You and Art were out with Gary tonight?

BREWSTER: Art was gonna tell you but I thought—

CONNIE: You thought you'd come and butter me up so I don't cause problems?

BREWSTER: Wait a minute.

CONNIE: Because it's not working.

BREWSTER: I know you're upset but I didn't know—

CONNIE: *(Cuts him off)* You're his best friend! Of course you did. Did Art write you too? "Dear Brews, Guess what? I'm marrying into the Longhouse—Don't tell Connie!"

BREWSTER: I'm your friend too—

CONNIE: Sure you are.

BREWSTER: Hey, don't blame this one me.

CONNIE: He's a real strategic thinker now, 'en he? "Of course, I can't be Longhouse, but heck, my kids can! Sorry we have to leave Connie in the dust but you'll help me tell her, won't you Brews!"

BREWSTER: I think they do love each other.

CONNIE: Aw, how sweet. Look at you Brews, trying to figure out ways to stop crazy Connie from wrecking things for her little brother.

BREWSTER: Maybe! You're practically foaming at the mouth!

CONNIE: I just found out my brother is marrying into the one family on the reservation that never have accepted us. They've never missed a chance to make me feel like dirt and now Art's marrying one of them!

BREWSTER: Why shouldn't he? You would've.

CONNIE: Asshole.

(Beat)

BREWSTER: I can understand why you're angry. I'm angry! It wasn't done right. That's why I came here. I wanted to tell you, so you can get angry. We can curse his ass out together but then when Art needs us to smile, we can.

CONNIE: Or maybe you just wanted to be the one to put the knife in.

BREWSTER: Oh Geez, Woman.

CONNIE: You do owe me a few, don't you?

BREWSTER: You are so—

CONNIE: Not sweet. *(She waves him out the door.)* Tick tock, Brews!

BREWSTER: Why do I even try?

(BREWSTER exits. CONNIE flops back on to the sofa. She pulls out a cigarette, FLINT pops up from behind the sofa and lights it.)

(End of scene)

Scene 6

(Lights up on the riverbank. The WOMAN supervises in back as FLINT prepares to offer the tobacco. But the tobacco is missing. He looks around, puzzled, the wooden bowl dangling carelessly from his fingers.)

(He searches around the stage. The WOMAN steps forward, and pulls the tobacco pouch out of her pocket, shows it to the audience, then replaces it.)

(Holding one finger up on her lip, she winks at the audience.)

WOMAN: No sacred offerings in front of non-Longhouse. Sorry! Nothing personal.

(The WOMAN steps back and to the side, gesturing to FLINT to follow her. "Teenage" CONNIE runs out. She carries a blanket and a large picnic basket. "Teenage" GARY strolls in behind her.)

(They can't see the WOMAN or FLINT.)

CONNIE: C'mon LAZY!

GARY: So what's this surprise?

CONNIE: I'm not gonna tell you…you gotta wait for it, that's part of the surprise! *(She starts setting up a picnic.)*

GARY: Can I guess…picnic?

CONNIE: Very funny. Don't be so impatient!

GARY: Well, at least let me help you.

CONNIE: You just can't sit still and let somebody spoil you, can you?

GARY: Well, why should you do all the work—

CONNIE: Relax and let me do the work, for a change.

GARY: Why?

CONNIE: Maybe you deserve it—ever think of that?

GARY: Nobody's ever done something like this for me before.

CONNIE: Well, that makes me special, doesn't it—now sit down and look pretty. If it makes you feel better, you're helping with clean-up.

GARY: Okay.

(GARY sits down on the blanket. He reaches over to give CONNIE a kiss but she pulls away.)

CONNIE: Later!

(GARY smiles and leans back on the blanket.)

GARY: So this is a famous Connie Farmer meal…

CONNIE: Famous?

GARY: Brews says you're practically gourmet.

CONNIE: Gourmet for Brews is barbequing at the river—so…

GARY: Take the compliment. He's not the only one.

CONNIE: Oh yeah? People are talking about me?

GARY: Lots of folks say you're good. Some even think you should go to chef's school—maybe open a restaurant.

CONNIE: Right. Sure I could.

GARY: I could help you—

CONNIE: Shhhhhh—shut your eyes. (*She ladles something into a cup.*) I don't need to go to culinary school to make this—

(GARY *takes a sip. Delicious. He sips again.*)

GARY: That's the best corn soup I've ever had!

CONNIE: Good! Now, I've got something else for you—

(CONNIE *pours something into a glass and holds it up for* GARY *to sip.*)

GARY: Okay…if it's half as good— (*He sips—his eyes open.*) Strawberry tea—

CONNIE: I know it's Strawberry Festival—

GARY: Yeah, um…it's really good—

(CONNIE *digs around in the basket, hands* GARY *a heavy biscuit.*)

GARY: Scawns—

CONNIE: Yeah, it's my Mom's recipe—

(CONNIE *grabs for more stuff—*GARY *stops her hand.*)

GARY: Connie, what are you trying to do?

CONNIE: What do you mean—

GARY: Cornsoup, Scawns, Strawberry Tea—

CONNIE: Yeah…

GARY: You've made me feast food.   Don't get me wrong, it's good but—

CONNIE: I don't know why it's a big deal—

GARY: What else you got in there, Con? Venison stew?

CONNIE: *(She shuts the basket.)* Nevermind, don't worry—you don't like it—you don't have to eat it—

GARY: Lemme see—*(He grabs the basket.)* Yep. Venison stew—

CONNIE: Like I said, if you don't like it, you don't have to eat it—

GARY: What else have you got in here— *(Pulls out another container.)* This is only supposed to be made by Medicine People—no one else. What are you trying to do here?

CONNIE: I thought you'd—I could show you I could help with ceremonies—

GARY: Connie we went over this. I told you from the start. You're not going to Longhouse with me.

(Beat)

CONNIE: We've been together for six months now.

GARY: So?

CONNIE: We belong together.

GARY: I'm gonna be a Chief. I can't have a wife who isn't Longhouse, you know that.

CONNIE: But—

GARY: I told you that the first time we went out.

CONNIE: But—when we made love, it was magical—

GARY: It was a mistake—

CONNIE: Didn't feel like one. Felt Perfect.

(CONNIE strokes GARY's hair. He pulls her hands off of him.)

GARY: Connie, will you back off!

CONNIE: Is it so wrong for us to be together? I like you. You like me, we always have a good time—I don't understand why.

GARY: Because it's not right. And it's not fair to you.

CONNIE: If you really wanted me, they could make me honorary.

GARY: What?!

CONNIE: They could make me a Longhouse—

GARY: Your mother was a Christian.

CONNIE: So? She converted.

GARY: She rejected everything we are for the Invaders—

CONNIE: Well, I didn't convert—

GARY: You were born Christian—you're born into the life you're supposed to have.

CONNIE: Right—mothers are everything to the "True-Indians" right? *(Beat)* I'm pregnant.

GARY: What?!

CONNIE: Wow. I would've thought they covered this in Longhouse. When a boy and a girl have sex, the sperm fertilizes the egg and—

GARY: *(Cuts her off)* So now we're having a kid—Right. I never thought you'd try this—

CONNIE: Excuse me?

GARY: I feel sorry for you.

CONNIE: No, feel sorry for your kid, because he or she won't be True-Indian, either!

GARY: You're a piece of work, you know that?

(GARY stalks off. CONNIE sits back on the blanket. FLINT sits down beside her, offers her some tobacco, She doesn't see him. He pats her stomach.)

WOMAN: *(Nods to audience)* Nothing personal.

(The WOMAN *strolls over and taps* FLINT *on the shoulder. Stubborn to the end he shakes his head. She waits, then snatches the bowl out of his hands, holding it above his head, she exits.* CONNIE *snaps out of it.)*

(End of scene)

END OF ACT ONE

ACT TWO

Scene 1

(Lights up on CONNIE's *livingroom. The* WOMAN *stands behind* CONNIE's *sofa.)*

*(*CONNIE *is seated in front of her, in the shadows, smoking. The* WOMAN *brushes* CONNIE's *hair as she speaks.* CONNIE *stays seated, as the* WOMAN *tells a story.)*

WOMAN: It was a woman who first accepted the Great Law of Peace. This is the law that binds us all together, and makes us all the Ongwehonwe, the one-people. The People of the Longhouse. She helped the Peacemaker persuade the Five Nations to accept the Peace. This is why, the Haudenosaunee come to the world through their Mothers.

(Lights up on CONNIE *and the* WOMAN *is in the shadows. The* WOMAN *continues to brush* CONNIE's *hair.)*

*(*CONNIE *picks up a picture of her parents from the coffee table.)*

CONNIE: *(To photo)* It's always sad to look at you. You were so happy. Didn't know what you were in for, did you? I can only remember moments; you brushing my hair, letting me lick the spoon when you made chocolate pudding, the day you painted my nails pink for me so we would match—silly little moments. Mom moments. And then you were gone. And Dad was—well, he was never the same.

Do you know who helped us? Longhouse people. They came over, they brought us food and took care of us until we got on our feet again. It was like having tons of Aunts and Uncles and all sorts of family, and then, when the job was finished, when their duty was over, they were gone, too. We no longer mattered.

(The WOMAN *stops brushing* CONNIE'*s hair and steps back.)*

CONNIE: It's really silly. It's just a simple wooden building. Strangers miss it. It looks like a storage shed. But, that simple building is the heart of this community. It's tradition and family. It's who we are. The doors were always open for Dad. Now they're open for Art. They just close when I get there. Not with a slam but lightly, like a gentle slap on the hand. I should know better. I should be happy. Sounds reasonable, doesn't it? Well, it pisses me off.

*(*BREWSTER *enters. He spots* CONNIE *and stops. She senses him, but continues to ignore him. Finally he pulls the flask out of his pocket and takes a swig.)*

*(*CONNIE, *still not looking, whips one of the sofa pillows at his head.)*

CONNIE: I've told you, no drinking in this house.

BREWSTER: Sure, take a man's last defense away from him. *(He caps the bottle and sits down.)*

CONNIE: Ugh! You stink like whiskey.

BREWSTER: Come on, I'm still smarting from the last visit.

CONNIE: Maybe you should stay away until you recover.

BREWSTER: And let you think you think you Beat me? No chance. Your brother wants to talk to you.

CONNIE: No.

BREWSTER: He doesn't want to hurt you.

CONNIE: Great, tell him to keep his girlfriend away from me.

BREWSTER: No.

CONNIE: What?

BREWSTER: He wants her, and she wants him. That's a good thing. He should get to have that.

CONNIE: You don't understand Brews, there's got to be an angle. Why would the Smokes allow the marriage?

BREWSTER: He's a War hero—he honors the Warrior tradition. Makes everyone proud. Besides it doesn't matter. It's all about the mother. You know that. Art and Karen's kids will be Longhouse.

CONNIE: I know what's going to happen. While the wedding is on, everything's going to be soooo sweet! All family together! After they've settled into the house, you and I will be invited over for dinner, or maybe a party or two. The kids will be running around playing and then somebody will look at me and remember. Some of them think I got rid of the baby.

BREWSTER: You're crazy but not crazy enough to lie about that shit—

CONNIE: Thanks.

BREWSTER: You're welcome.

CONNIE: They made up their minds long ago. They don't believe I lost it. Either I got rid of it or I made it up to make him marry me. They'll start working on Art and pretty soon, my invitations will stop.

BREWSTER: He won't let that happen.

CONNIE: And poor Uncle Brewster! What happens the first time Karen smells liquor on your breath? Will she let you around the kids?

BREWSTER: You really make this supportive crap hard, you know?

CONNIE: I'm just giving you a heads up. Art is moving beyond us.

BREWSTER: He did that when he ran away and joined the war. Don't kid yourself.

CONNIE: So my little brother decided being in a war zone was better than being here.

BREWSTER: I don't know—I can see how it would appeal. You can see the bullets over there.

CONNIE: Such an asshole.

BREWSTER: You love me.

(ARTHUR SR *enters,* ART *follows close on his heels.*)

ARTHUR SR: Still in one piece, huh?

BREWSTER: I'm quicker than I look.

CONNIE: I'm glad you all find this so funny.

ART: I'm not laughing.

CONNIE: Why didn't you tell me, Dad?

ART: I wanted to tell you myself—

CONNIE: Dad?

ARTHUR SR: It wasn't my place.

ART: It's my marriage. My wife—my job to tell you.

CONNIE: Well, you didn't, did you—I can't believe you got through the war being such a bald-faced chicken.

ART: Do yourself a favor and don't talk about stuff that you don't understand.

CONNIE: Well, that's everything, isn't it?

BREWSTER: You're making it too easy, man.

CONNIE: Shut up Brews. I'm talking to my little brother.

ART: No you're not you're yelling, like you always do—hoping that the rest of us will give up and let you have your way. I'm not so easily intimidated anymore.

CONNIE: Says the "War hero!"

ART: Will stop about that shit! Leave it alone!

CONNIE: Why? I was just talking about sending Brews to do your dirty work for you. What are you talking about?

ART: Nevermind.

ARTHUR SR: Constance, you should be happy for your brother—this, getting married—it's a good step.

CONNIE: Right, because we're all friends now and even Gary's celebrating.

ARTHUR SR: You two were over long ago. Its time to move on. You said you wanted change—do something about it. Maybe forgiving Gary could be a good first step.

CONNIE: Forget about the baby, too, I suppose.

ARTHUR SR: Time's passing, Sweetheart. Fixate on that one baby you lost and you soon you'll run out of time to have others.

CONNIE: Sure, why didn't I think of that, just get pregnant. Have a baby or maybe six. It'll keep me busy, won't it.

ARTHUR SR: Keep you out of trouble, that's for sure.

CONNIE: I can't believe you said that, Dad.

ARTHUR SR: Look, have kids or don't have kids—I just want you to start thinking of possibilities.

CONNIE: Like marry Brews, you mean?

BREWSTER: Woah, what?

ARTHUR SR: I wasn't saying that.

CONNIE: That's exactly what you were saying last night. *(To* BREWSTER*)* Dad was planning to set us up—take care of two problems in one. That way NEITHER of us is in Art's way.

ARTHUR SR: That wasn't what I meant, young lady. I'm worried about you—all you've got is your job and your house and okay maybe I did think that you and Brewster—

BREWSTER: Mr Farmer—

ARTHUR SR: —and yes Brewster, I worry about you too. You just quit your last job and you've got nothing lined up but that whiskey in your pocket and maybe I did think for a moment that it would be something, for both of you—because you both do need something. But that was about you, Constance because I love you, and you too Brews, because I worry, and I don't know how such a good kid—a kid with all the gifts in the world—

BREWSTER: also has a gift for disappointing everybody?

ARTHUR SR: That wasn't what I was saying.

BREWSTER: Everybody says it, at some time or another. I didn't expect it here, but that's okay.

ARTHUR SR: You're a good kid, Brews.

BREWSTER: Good enough to marry your daughter?

CONNIE: Hah! Not likely.

ARTHUR SR: Constance!

(Beat)

BREWSTER: Well, hell, that's my cue.

ART: No, man—come on—stay. You're my back up.

CONNIE: Thought you didn't need Brewster around to do your dirty work?

BREWSTER: Relax Connie—I get it. You don' want me around. I'm gone. *(Bows to the room)* It's been so nice visiting—but I really must jet. *(He exits, pulling out his flask.)*

ART: That wasn't cool.

ARTHUR SR: He's a tough kid, he'll be alright.

CONNIE: Is it cool that he's killing himself and we all don't say anything? Why, because he's funny? He's a drunk—

ART: He's not—

CONNIE: No, He just drinks all the time—that's all.

ART: Geez, Connie, you're like a battering ram, you just get people cornered and you keep hammering.

CONNIE: It would be so much easier if I just let things slide, like you huh?

ART: I don't let things slide—

CONNIE: Or have you forgotten it all? Have you forgotten that the Smokes are the family that made it hell on earth for us here? That Gary used to be the one who would lock us out of the school, that he and his cronies used to throw mud and rocks at us when we walked down the street. We had to go everywhere together because you were so scared…do you remember that, Art?

ARTHUR SR: What? Why didn't you tell me?

CONNIE: You had enough to deal with Dad. This was ours.

ART: I remember—and I remember that when Brewster found out, he started walking with us—scared them all off. He also Beat up Gary when he pushed you off the tire swing. Nice way to pay him back today.

CONNIE: He needs to start hearing the truth. We all need a little more truth around here.

ART: Karen wasn't like Gary.

CONNIE: Well, she was nice to you—you were a baby, and kind of adorable. She was a bitch to me—everyday.

ARTHUR SR: I wish you two had come to me—

CONNIE: What could you do? Mom had just died.

ARTHUR SR: I could've helped. Kids are always horrible to each other but I could've helped. Helped to talk you through it—helped you defend yourselves.

ART: It was okay, Dad.

ARTHUR SR: No its not. Not if we're still hearing about it.

CONNIE: We're still hearing about it because it never stopped.

ART: Because you won't let it! What am I supposed to do, Connie? Am I supposed to stay here and live with you and fixate on shit that happened years ago? You may want to spend the rest of your life like that, but I'm not gonna.

CONNIE: Go and marry your Longhouse Princess, then—let's see what happens.

ART: Don't you get it? Once Karen and I are married—

CONNIE: What? We're all gonna be friends? All go to ceremonies together?

ART: You won't even give me a chance, will ya? I can make them understand!

CONNIE: Karen listens to you, does she? Big man?

ART: If you just bend. They might bend. They know we're part of this community.

CONNIE: But not True-Indian.

ART: No. Because we're not. That doesn't mean that we can't find our place here, right?

CONNIE: Why are you even asking me? You've got it all figured out.

(Beat)

ART: Yeah, why I am asking? *(He exits.)*

ARTHUR SR: You should've told me.

CONNIE: Are you really so surprised, Dad? You must've know what would happen when you married a Christian.

ARTHUR SR: You're right. I should've thought about that. But instead I thought, she's good-hearted and kind I want her to be the mother of my kids. That was my mistake. Very selfish.

CONNIE: No. That's not what I'm saying.

ARTHUR SR: Really? Sounds to me you're ashamed of your mother. And me, for marrying her.

CONNIE: No, Dad. I know you loved her. I just don't think you realized that when you did that—you would be having two kids that weren't Longhouse.

ARTHUR SR: No, you're right. I was hoping I'd have two kids that were healthy, happy and as beautiful as their mother. Again, my mistake.

CONNIE: Forget it, you don't understand.

ARTHUR SR: What I understand is that your brother got back from that place in one piece, when lots of other folks are dying quick out there. He's come back to start his life with a good woman who loves him. These are good things.

CONNIE: Look at the big picture and smile like a good girl.. Don't worry about losing my family because it's all for the greater good.

ARTHUR SR: I've always been proud of you. I was worried when your Mom passed that I wouldn't be able to raise a good strong daughter. Indian women have to be strong. But you're so rigid—you have to be careful. Rigid is easy to break.

(End of scene)

Scene 2

(The riverbank. The WOMAN *is seated on a folding chair, a blanket is folded over her lap. She balances bunch of tobacco leaves in her lap. Carefully, she binds them, preparing them for drying.)*

WOMAN: *(To audience)* When Tobacco is taken from the earth, you know it's good. All prepared by hand, the Right Way. Real tobacco isn't sold in smoke shops or in tins, it isn't rolled up in little papers and poisoned with nicotine. Tobacco is one of the most sacred plants Because its roots go deep into the earth and it's smoke rises high into the sky.

*(*CONNIE *enters. She lingers upstage, watching as the* WOMAN *works.)*

WOMAN: *(As* MRS SMOKE*)* Constance Marie Farmer. *(She stops working. Carefully, she folds the blanket up, taking care not to bruise the leaves.)*

CONNIE: Hello Mrs Smoke.

WOMAN: *(As* MRS SMOKE*)* No need to hide. I don't bite. We're gonna be family, I can't have you hiding at the dinner table.

*(*CONNIE *steps forward, hesitantly.)*

WOMAN: *(As* MRS SMOKE*)* Still pretty as ever, I see.

CONNIE: Thank you. Were you just preparing tobacco?

WOMAN: *(As* MRS SMOKE*)* Yes. *(She waits, smiles—does nothing.)*

CONNIE: Don't let me stop you. I'm not going to taint it or anything.

WOMAN: *(As* MRS SMOKE*)* Still smoking cigarettes?

CONNIE: Yeah, but everybody does.

WOMAN: *(As* MRS SMOKE*)* Not everybody. It'll make you old before your time, and your breath will smell bad. Boys won't mind right now, but give it a few years. Yellow teeth, stinky breath. That's less forgivable when you're in your forties.

CONNIE: Mrs Smoke, I, uh, think we should talk.

WOMAN: *(As* MRS SMOKE*)* Extra wrinkles come too.

CONNIE: Can I talk to you?

WOMAN: *(As* MRS SMOKE*)* Of course. What would you like to talk about?

CONNIE: My brother marrying Karen.

WOMAN: *(As* MRS SMOKE*)* Oh.

CONNIE: He believes you support it.

WOMAN: *(As* MRS SMOKE*)* He's right.

CONNIE: But you can't be happy about this!

WOMAN: *(As* MRS SMOKE*)* Why not? I like Art. Don't you?

CONNIE: It's not that! Not at all! Of course I do—Art's my brother. Despite hanging out with Brewster all the time—

WOMAN: *(As* MRS SMOKE*)* You hang out with Brewster all the time.

CONNIE: Well, yeah, but I don't go drinking with him—

WOMAN: *(As* MRS SMOKE*)* Art assures me he wants to adopt traditional ways.

CONNIE: He just went out with Brewster the other night.

WOMAN: *(As* MRS SMOKE*)* Got in a fight too, didn't they?

CONNIE: Yep!

WOMAN: *(As* MRS SMOKE*)* As I recall, Art's the one who ended up with bruises.

CONNIE: Exactly!

WOMAN: *(As* MRS SMOKE*)* Just want to sink him, don't ya?

CONNIE: No—I thought you should know!

WOMAN: *(As* MRS SMOKE*)* I knew already. They told me what happened.

CONNIE: I mean, isn't it important? He gets in barroom brawls? That's not very traditional.

WOMAN: *(As* MRS SMOKE*)* Did you know the fight was all about you? Your Brewster and my Gary exchanged words. Your brother was trying to make peace.

CONNIE: Peacemaker! I get it. Wow, he's perfect for the Longhouse, ain't he?

WOMAN: *(As* MRS SMOKE*)* Starting to sound bitter now too. Yellow teeth, stinky breath, wrinkles and bitter. You'd better get a fella soon.

CONNIE: I'm trying to discuss something serious here!

WOMAN: *(As* MRS SMOKE*)* No, you're not. You're trying to make trouble. You don't care who Karen marries as long as it's not Art, isn't that it? What would your mother say?

CONNIE: How do you know what my mother would think? It's not like you two were friends.

WOMAN: *(As* MRS SMOKE*)* She was an honorable woman. She would never want you to ruin your brother's happiness, especially when there's no reason.

CONNIE: Yeah, well maybe she'd understand. Maybe she would appreciate not being related to the man who dumped me after making me pregnant.

WOMAN: *(As* MRS SMOKE*)* Pregnant, huh?

CONNIE: Yes! Pregnant!

WOMAN: *(As* MRS SMOKE*)* The baby didn't come. So either you got rid of it or …

CONNIE: I lost it! Like I said!

WOMAN: *(As* MRS SMOKE*)* Yes, like you said. Like you said you were pregnant. If the baby had come, Gary would've taken care of it. Would've raised the child to know it's home and it's place here on the reservation.

CONNIE: And what place is that?

WOMAN: *(As* MRS SMOKE*)* Fireside, with his family.

CONNIE: But there'd be barriers.

WOMAN: *(As* MRS SMOKE*)* Yes. There are. This is how it is.

CONNIE: It used to be different. People could be adopted in. Special people, politicians, honorary family members, all could be adopted in.

WOMAN: *(As* MRS SMOKE*)* Rarely and always, it had to be earned. One of the first lessons learned, was that the more we shared with the Invaders, the more we'd lose. Started doing trade with them and learned their language so we could deal with them. Next thing you know, our language started disappearing.
Invite them to a ceremony to do them honor and they take the ceremonies and sell it to others as entertainment—like a puppet show. The sacredness was lost. And when we gave them the great gift of tobacco, what happened? In their hands, our medicine turns the young, old.

CONNIE: I'm not one of them! I was born here. I was raised here.

WOMAN: *(As* MRS SMOKE*)* And for all that, you should know better than anyone. Every Haudenosaunee knows there's a place for everyone on the Mother. Trouble only happens when people try be something they're not meant to be.

CONNIE: You've never liked me, did you?

(The WOMAN *stands up, cradling the blanket.)*

WOMAN: *(As* MRS SMOKE*)* I like your spunk. I don't like your anger. I don't like that it's aimed at your own people.

(Beat)

CONNIE: You baked cookies.

WOMAN: *(As* MRS SMOKE*)* Pardon?

CONNIE: At my mother's wake. You let me lick the spoon.

WOMAN: *(As* MRS SMOKE*)* That's right. *(She exits.)*

(End of scene)

Scene 3

*(*CONNIE*'s livingroom. She stacks some cookies onto a plate and sets it on the coffee table. She paces around, plumping the pillows on the sofa.)*

(The bell rings. The door opens, and GARY *takes one step into the room.)*

CONNIE: Hi. How are you?

GARY: Sorry. I don't have that much time. You said it was urgent?

CONNIE: Don't I rate a hello, at least?

GARY: Hello.

CONNIE: Take a seat. Please.

GARY: How can I help you?

CONNIE: I was hoping we could be friendly.

Gary strolls all the way in. He sits on the edge of the sofa ready to bolt.

GARY: Okay?

CONNIE: Great. Good. Would you like something to drink?

GARY: Can we get to the point, please?

CONNIE: I'm a little bit shocked about Karen and Art.

GARY: Of course you are but I don't think you need to worry. I think Art's got things figured out.

CONNIE: So you think he's marrying Karen just to get into the Longhouse.

GARY: Is that what you think?

CONNIE: Come on Gary— All they did was write letters. Art hasn't even been back a week yet.

GARY: They spent his last leave together.

CONNIE: He said he wasn't getting any leave because he was almost done his tour—

GARY: Like I said, he knows what he's doing.

(Beat)

CONNIE: Why are you letting it happen?

GARY: He's my sister's choice. And a warrior. He's an honor to any family.

CONNIE: You really want a Christian in your family? *(Beat)* Of course, because it doesn't matter who his mother was, does it? The kids will be Longhouse.

GARY: I'm not stopping the wedding. My sister is happy.

CONNIE: You don't miss me at all do you?

GARY: What's my favorite color?

CONNIE: Pardon me?

GARY: My favorite food?

CONNIE: I don't know—burgers?

GARY: My favorite band? Favorite Movie? Favorite book?

(CONNIE *doesn't respond.*)

GARY: You didn't love me, Connie. You barely know me.

CONNIE: Why because I don't know your favorite color?

GARY: All you cared about was Longhouse. It was all questions about ceremonies and becoming Chief. Did you know I play guitar? I was in a band for a couple of years—still play with them sometimes on weekends. I also love football. Can even recite stats. Superbowl weekend at the house is crazy. Any of this interesting to you? No. I didn't think so—

CONNIE: You're trying to turn yourself into some kind of victim.

GARY: There were no victims with you and me. And you're not going to make my sister one. Or Art. Not while I'm around.

CONNIE: Say what you want, Art knows me.

GARY: So do I. Your favorite color is Candy Apple red. When you were little you used to daydream about being a singer in a slinky dress on TV. Your favorite movie is *The Philadelphia Story*—you like the banter but it's really because of how gentle they all are in the end. I like cheese on my burgers, by the way.

CONNIE: How sweet. You have a good memory. I'm sorry that you think I've forgotten you. I haven't. How's this? You told me once, that it was families like ours that ruined the reservation.

You said that people like us should go where we
belonged, and that my Dad was a traitor to his people.
That people were only nice to us because they had to
be and that really they would rather us go away.

GARY: Connie—

CONNIE: Oh, and my favorite! Um, let's see…I think
it was, yes—what a good thing it was that my mother
died, because it was one less Christian traitor on the
reservation. Yeah, that one was my favorite.

GARY: I was a kid.

CONNIE: You were fourteen? Old enough to be a
"warrior".

(GARY gets up to leave.)

CONNIE: And then—just a few years later—you
stopped calling me names. You smiled at me. You told
me I was pretty. Even though the whole reservation
knew, you took me out. For the first time I felt like I
belonged.

GARY: You do belong. Just not with me.

CONNIE: Right. I forgot.

Gary turns to leave, but stops.

GARY: Are you ever going to tell me the truth?

CONNIE: What?

GARY: Was there ever a baby?

CONNIE: A little Christian baby? What do you care?

(End of scene)

Scene 4

(The bar. GARY *is eating. An almost empty beer is sitting in front of him.* BREWSTER *enters, gets a shot and a beer from* FLINT *and spots* GARY—FLINT *follows close behind playing with the buckskin bag. During this scene,* FLINT *messes with* GARY, *stealing food—giving him his drinks etc.)*

BREWSTER: Wow, this place has gone to hell in a handbasket. I mean, what sort of place lets a Longhouse hang out drinking? It's downright immoral, don't you think? What would Handsome Lake think?

GARY: Not today, Brewster.

BREWSTER: *(Sitting)* I don't see why not. I wouldn't be good Haudenosaunee if I let this one go.

GARY: You're not a good Haudenosaunee.

BREWSTER: Yeah, well—

GARY: Once, in a while, I like a beer. Just one. And my sister's getting married! I think I'm allowed to celebrate. *(He drains the beer.)*

BREWSTER: Celebrating, huh? You look like you need another one. Or something stronger.

GARY: I'm fine.

BREWSTER: Nope—something tells me that having the Farmers join "the family" isn't going down as easy as that beer is.

GARY: A Warrior is a honor to any household.

BREWSTER: Bullshit. You just want a reason to hang around Connie.

GARY: No, that would be you.

*(*BREWSTER *drains the shot in his hand.)*

BREWSTER: Hits the spot. You should get one.

GARY: Sometimes Brews, I swear you do it, just to piss everybody off.

BREWSTER: It's weird, first you hate them, then you date Connie and now you're cool with Art?

GARY: Mr Farmer's family has been Ongwehonwe for generations.

BREWSTER: So was Mrs Farmer's.

GARY: She abandoned her beliefs to become a Christian.

BREWSTER: So if you feel that way, why are you okay with Art?

GARY: I told you—

BREWSTER: A Warrior? Its such bullshit— This isn't our war, it's not our conflict. Why should any Indian volunteer to help them?

GARY: You forget about the treaties. We gave our word. We promised warriors to our allies.

BREWSTER: Bullshit— Treaties? We don't have any left, man, they broke every single one!

GARY: Exactly. THEY DID. They broke their oath, they don't respect us, and they think that absolves them of any responsibility. What does it show them when we do what they do? If we don't follow through on our word? We're people of Honor.

BREWSTER: Nice speech. You are starting to sound like a Clan Chief. Instead of an asshole—is all I'm saying.

GARY: Art is a man of honor—he makes us all proud. I know this is a difficult concept for you—

BREWSTER: Yeah, you're so honorable, you screwed over a pregnant chick.

GARY: That's between me and Connie but I can tell you— If I'd promised her anything, it would've been done. I didn't lie to or mislead her.

BREWSTER: Right. Sometime tonight, you know you're gonna get a second beating, right?

GARY: Lookit who's all honorable now—

BREWSTER: I know about honor—

GARY: Yeah? Starting to remember who you were supposed to be?

BREWSTER: Don't start that shit again.

GARY: I'm not the only one at this table who was supposed to be a Chief.

BREWSTER: Yeah? Because the Clan Mothers say so?

GARY: Yeah. They said from the moment you could talk they knew you were a born leader. What are you afraid of Brews?

(BREWSTER *waves to* FLINT *and he brings over two shots. He hands one to* GARY, *who accepts it, reluctantly.*)

BREWSTER: I'm afraid I'd be wound as tightly as you are now. I'm afraid I'd be the kind of man who'd screw over the girl I loved because she wasn't raised traditionally. Cheers—

GARY: The girl, I love, huh? I'm not the one who keeps bringing her up, here.

BREWSTER: Drink that. You need more liquor in your life.

GARY: Could you quit being such a stereotype— please. (*He downs the shot.*) And just for the record— you do realize that I was the one who gave you the beatdown—last time.

BREWSTER: Well, Cheers, Chief!

(B*REWSTER* *waves to* F*LINT* *who brings over two more shots.*)

(*End of scene*)

Scene 5

(*Later.* C*ONNIE* *has her feet up on the table beside the plate of stale cookies.* F*LINT* *sits beside her, eating them.*)

(*There is a knock, and* K*AREN* *pushes open the door.*)

K*AREN*: Hello? Oh, Hi Connie. Is Art around?

C*ONNIE*: Do you see him?

K*AREN*: I thought he was visiting you?

C*ONNIE*: He was. We had a fight.

K*AREN*: I'm sorry to hear that.

C*ONNIE*: Are you?

K*AREN*: I'm sorry for Art. This is hard for him. He doesn't want to have to choose between us.

C*ONNIE*: So don't make him.

K*AREN*: I'm not. (*Beat*) You were a very good sister to him.

C*ONNIE*: Well, I had to be, didn't I?

K*AREN*: I'll be a good wife to him. Why not start over with us?

C*ONNIE*: Like Gary?

K*AREN*: Gary has accepted him. He could accept you too.

C*ONNIE*: I'm sure your whole family is thrilled.

K*AREN*: We don't bite. Come to dinner with us!

C*ONNIE*: Yeah, you can spare me that one.

(*Beat*)

KAREN: You know, I've always wondered, why do you want to be Haudenosaunee so much? It's clear you hate us—

(Beat)

CONNIE: Why do I want to be a part of my own culture? Wow, it was either brains or beauty for you, huh? How would you feel if you were told you couldn't be a member of the Smoke family anymore.

KAREN: I'm gonna be nice because I love Art and I want what's best for him, but let me answer a couple of things you said. I would be horrified if I woke up and was kicked out of my family. That's why we shun people as a punishment. It's horrible not to be able to be with the people you love, and I'd hate it. Because I'd already been a member—I was born a member of that family and it would be mine to lose.

CONNIE: You're so smug—look at you. Ms Six Nations, 1998! You wouldn't know what it's like to have your identity denied you.

KAREN: It's not your identity. It's mine. The same way I'm part of my mother's Clan, the same way I'm a brown-haired Mohawk and not a tall blonde from Sweden. In the same way that you are someone with Tuscarora blood who was born to a Christian Woman and a Longhouse man.

CONNIE: So why'd the creator put me here? To get in everyone's face? And Art, was he put here to be a back-up husband for the Princess in case she couldn't maintain any of her others...oh, and she couldn't could she?

KAREN: Trying to get me to doubt Art? He knows what he wants Look how he's breaking away from you. He's spent all his life jumping to your tune but he's not going to be jumping for you anymore. Around me, he's a grown man.

CONNIE: Are you so sure he would be around if you weren't Longhouse?

KAREN: You know, if you really respected Longhouse—

CONNIE: Who says I do?

KAREN: You do. Everytime you ask about it. Everytime you wave a bit of smudge around, or every time you make your strawberry tea—you say you care. But the truth is that if you really respected Longhouse, you would respect the law.

CONNIE: And not try to fight for my rights?

KAREN: They're not your rights! You're not fighting City Hall. You're fighting against the Great Law. *(Beat)* You know, you're right to be worried—bout me and Art. He's gonna learn who we are, and what's gonna happen is that he is gonna see you for who you really are. Think about it.

You want what doesn't belong to you. You want to go somewhere you haven't been invited and you won't be welcomed. You want to push your way in with little respect for our traditions or our beliefs. *(Beat)* You're our very own Manifest Destiny incarnated—and you wonder why we keep our distance.

CONNIE: Get out of my house.

KAREN: Tell Art I stopped by. Never mind—I'll tell him myself. Bye.

(KAREN exits. Beat. ART comes forward from kitchen area.)

CONNIE: You see now?

(End of scene)

Scene 6

(Thunder and lightning. Sounds of rainstorm. The WOMAN *runs in from stage left, obviously annoyed. Sighing, starts to search around the set, picking at the pieces.)*

WOMAN: *(To the audience)* You know, I turn my back on him for five minutes and boom! He's gone, and he's taken the pouch with him. I knew he was getting antsy.

(Sound of thunder)

WOMAN: The Thunderers are upset. They think I should've seen the signs. Bad Mind. Every day he's got to prove it.

(Thunder again. The WOMAN *makes a face.)*

WOMAN: *(Yelling at the storm)* Oh shut up already, I'm looking! *(Runs around the stage)* Flint! Flint! Get back here now! And give me back my sacred tobacco!

(Vignettes)

(Spotlight on BREWSTER *as he enters and the* WOMAN *exits. He sits down by the riverside.)*

(Thunder strike.)

(Spotlight up on ART, *still upset. Thunder strike.)*

(Spotlight up on GARY, *standing outside of* CONNIE's *door.)*

(Thunder strike.)

(Spotlight up on CONNIE, *smoking.)*

(Lights down)

END OF ACT TWO

ACT THREE

Scene 1

(More thunder and lightning. It's a heavy storm. Lightning illuminates a spotlight centerstage. FLINT is there. He chuckles as he pulls out the tobacco bowl from his pocket. Making a shushing gesture toward the audience, he sets down the bowl. Smiling he pulls a cigarette out from it and lights it. He takes a couple quick puffs and throws the cigarette over his shoulder. Lightning strikes again and then blackout. There is the crackling of the fire and the spotlight goes up on the Longhouse. It's on fire.)

(Blackout, end of scene)

Scene 2

(Lights up on the riverbank. BREWSTER is seated downstage center. He stares across the river. CONNIE enters and heads over to him.)

CONNIE: Isn't your rear getting a soaker?

BREWSTER: I'll just fortify against the damp. *(He reaches into his pocket and pulls out his flask. He takes a long sip.)*

CONNIE: Brewster, come on—it's early.

BREWSTER: Or very late, depending.

CONNIE: Put it away, will you? I want to talk.

BREWSTER: *(Brandishing the flask)* Handy little thing, this. Keeps things safe, and is kinda discreet-like. Fits in the pocket, nicely. Kinda classy. I'm nothing if not a classy guy. *(Takes another sip)* Kinda cliche ennit? Here sits an Indian, drinking.

(CONNIE glares at BREWSTER.)

CONNIE: You should be Longhouse, Con, that's the exact look they all give me. They'd like to pretend Indians don't drink. I know that's why they all pretend I'm not here. But you don't get to.

CONNIE: I'm not—I just hate seeing you do that to yourself.

BREWSTER: You came here for a reason, right?

CONNIE: Yeah, I—uh…

BREWSTER: If this is an apology, I need a fortifying sip. Okay, shoot—

CONNIE: Brews, I really am sorry. Sometimes I don't think.

BREWSTER: That's true.

CONNIE: I shouldn't have spoken to you like that.

BREWSTER: Nope.

CONNIE: You always have my back and I—

BREWSTER: I got it. You're sorry.

CONNIE: I just—I can't believe they don't get what's going on here. They don't see it! But I do. You know what I'm talking about. You don't think I'm crazy.

BREWSTER: Well, of course you're crazy. That's a given.

(CONNIE sticks her tongue out.)

BREWSTER: Promises, promises…

I know what you're saying. For all your brother's best intentions, I know he'll feel the strain every time you come over for dinner and Gary is there. And there's gonna be a day when Art is embarrassed by me. Heck, you already are.

CONNIE: Not embarrassed.

BREWSTER: Disappointed, though—right?

(CONNIE shrugs.)

BREWSTER: Always that one. *(He drains the flask.)* Damn, it's empty. Anyways, what I was saying is, this will all happen, if they stay together.

CONNIE: What?

BREWSTER: Art is gonna have to do all the work, here. He's the one who has to learn traditional ways. He's the one who has to move into her home. He's the one who will suddenly have to pay attention to Gary. Don't you think that will bug him?

CONNIE: He'll be with the woman he loves, and he'll be with the Longhouses.

BREWSTER: He won't like owing them. I think they've even lined him up a job. In Gary's company.

CONNIE: So, he's getting a wife, a house, and a career in one afternoon.

BREWSTER: All because Gary snapped his fingers. You think he's gonna like that? He's still your brother. See how he likes it if Gary talks shit about you.

CONNIE: I don't want him to fight them because of me.

BREWSTER: But you don't want him marrying her.

CONNIE: Just because I think it will be horrible for him.

BREWSTER: He needs to find out on his own. You've said what you can, and now, just sit back and see what happens. I have a feeling it might not. They haven't really been with each other very much. Its possible it might not happen. If it does, who's to say it won't collapse in a few months?

Especially with Karen's track record.

CONNIE: So if I wait it out, all will be good?

BREWSTER: Well, not if you're gonna be a bitch about the wedding. You'll give him reason to fight to stay in it and when it does fail, he could blame you. Be nice, and he'll run right back to the family when its done.

CONNIE: So I change my mind, just like that?

BREWSTER: You love your brother and only want what's best for him. Trust me, they'll buy it. They want to. Really badly.

CONNIE: Slick, you are slick.

BREWSTER: And here, you thought I was just another pretty face.

CONNIE: True, very true. Lemme look. *(She grabs his chin.)* Beyond pretty, I'd say. Those eyes are something. If they weren't bleary, I could stare into them for hours. Nice broad shoulders, plenty of strength to lean on. Very sexy mouth— *(She leans forward)* —pity it reeks of whiskey.

(CONNIE pushes BREWSTER away.)

BREWSTER: You love driving me crazy, don't you?

CONNIE: Yep.

BREWSTER: Why?

CONNIE: Use your brain. It used to be a good one.

(GARY enters.)

GARY: You Bitch! If you were a man I'd—

BREWSTER: I'm a man—say what you gotta say—

GARY: *(To CONNIE)* Why would you do it? How could you do it? It's families, grandmothers, people who never did anything to you! You claim we're your people! How could you?!

CONNIE: What are you talking about?!

(ART *enters.*)

ART: I told you, there's no way she did it!

BREWSTER: What the hell is going on?

GARY: I haven't heard her deny it!

CONNIE: Deny what?! Will somebody please tell me what happened?

ART: The Longhouse burned down.

CONNIE: Oh no!

BREWSTER: And you come looking for her? Fuck you— she didn't do it.

GARY: Right. No way she'd get rid of the baby and no way she'd burn down the Longhouse.

BREWSTER: It is possible it's an accident. There was a storm last night.

GARY: There was rain, too. A natural extinguisher.

CONNIE: You gotta believe me—I didn't do this.

ART: The timber of the Longhouse was old, it could've gone anytime!

GARY: Even after rainstorm. Got lucky again, didn't you?

CONNIE: What are you talking about?

GARY: Timing is perfect, isn't it? You know we'd never let Karen marry into the family of the woman who burned down our Longhouse.

ART: I know I've been going along to get along, but don't come here and accuse my sister and expect me to do nothing.

GARY: So much for my new "brother" huh? *(To* CONNIE*)* Really clever—very smart.

*(*ART *goes for* GARY, *but* BREWSTER *holds him back.)*

BREWSTER: Not true, Gary. Connie doesn't want to stop the wedding anymore, do you, Connie?

CONNIE: No! I changed my mind. I was ready to try and be friends.

GARY: *(Sarcastic)* Oh, of course.

ART: Really? After what Karen said—

CONNIE: It doesn't matter. I want my little brother happy. I want my family happy. I was ready to try.

GARY: You're good, I'll give you that.

CONNIE: Obviously, it's too much to hope. Something goes wrong, and it's my fault, again. Something horrible happens and it must be because I'm here.

GARY: You reap what you sow. And this time, you've taken down your family with you. Congratulations. I'll be seeing you all, later.

BREWSTER: Not if I see you first, asshole.

*(*GARY *exits.)*

ART: Connie—you alright?

*(*CONNIE *nods.)*

ART: I've gotta catch him before he gets to the Clan Mothers. *(He exits.)*

BREWSTER: Come on, Connie. I'll walk you home.

CONNIE: No—its okay. I'm okay. You go on, Brews.

*(*BREWSTER *exits. She stands there for a moment, staring off into the water.)*

CONNIE: Well, hell. Here we go.

(End of scene)

Scene 3

(CONNIE's *livingroom. The* WOMAN *[as* MRS SMOKE*)* is seated on a chair, having strawberry tea and cookies with ARTHUR SR *There's an odd aura of calm about the domestic scene.*)

WOMAN: *(As* MRS SMOKE*)* Constance makes a nice strawberry tea.

ARTHUR SR: She does.

WOMAN: *(As* MRS SMOKE*)* Like her mom, then? A knack with the cooking?

ARTHUR SR: Yeah. Try the cookies.

WOMAN: *(As* MRS SMOKE*)* Don't mind if I do. *(She samples one, it's delicious.)* So good! She should do something with this talent. Would be nice to have an Indian cooking show out there.

ARTHUR SR: Cooking show!

WOMAN: *(As* MRS SMOKE*)* Gary said she always wanted to be on TV.

ARTHUR SR: Heck, doesn't everybody? I wanna be on TV.

WOMAN: *(As* MRS SMOKE*)* Let me guess, Dancing with the Stars.

ARTHUR SR: Naw, something SciFi—

WOMAN: *(As* MRS SMOKE*)* Shame. I remember those fancy moves of yours—

ARTHUR SR: Oh yeah?

WOMAN: *(As* MRS SMOKE*)* We all wanted to dance with you.

ARTHUR SR: Well you never asked me.

WOMAN: *(As* MRS SMOKE*)* I guess I missed my chance. That' happens sometimes. *(Beat)* My Gary's convinced she did it.

ARTHUR SR: I can't believe that. I won't.

WOMAN: *(As* MRS SMOKE*)* I understand. But its strange that it would burn so quickly. So much of it gone! Seems suspicious.

ARTHUR SR: I raised my daughter to respect the Ongwehonwe. She would never.

WOMAN: *(As* MRS SMOKE*)* She's so angry. Your girl.

ARTHUR SR: Her biggest fear is losing family. She would never burn down the Longhouse. It's family.

WOMAN: *(As* MRS SMOKE*)* True. She does love her family.

ARTHUR SR: I tell you, there's no way it would be her.

WOMAN: *(As* MRS SMOKE*)* She's got real talent with her cooking. Everybody says so. Pity there's no where here for her to shine. She should go to the city. Lots of opportunities for a good cook in the city.

ARTHUR SR: She lives here.

WOMAN: *(As* MRS SMOKE*)* She's never been comfortable here. Don't be selfish. Let the girl go live her life. You'll still have Art. And Karen.

ARTHUR SR: So you're not stopping the wedding?

WOMAN: *(As* MRS SMOKE*)* Why would I? Karen's happy. Art's happy. It would be nice to see Connie happy too.

ARTHUR SR: I can't just say she's gonna go.

WOMAN: *(As* MRS SMOKE*)* Oh, I know. But you should talk to her. It just might be what that girl needs. Give her a place to direct her energies.

ARTHUR SR: I'd miss her.

WOMAN: (As MRS SMOKE) Just get Art to drive you. He'll want to visit her too. Or maybe that Brewster. I know he'll be over there.

ARTHUR SR: I don't know—

(The WOMAN rises, smiling. ARTHUR SR rises with her, escorting her to the front door.)

WOMAN: (As MRS SMOKE) Might be just the thing. And we can finally have our dance at the wedding.

(ARTHUR SR shuts the door. He pauses then stretches out on the sofa and stares at the ceiling, thinking.)

(ART and KAREN slam into the room. He doesn't move, and they don't notice him at first.)

KAREN: Okay. I'm here, I'm listening.

ART: I know she didn't do it.

KAREN: When I talked to her, it was clear. She didn't want this wedding.

ART: Yeah? What else was clear when you two were talking?

KAREN: What?

ART: Why are you marrying me?

KAREN: What kind of question is that? I love you.

ART: You love Manifest Destiny?

(Beat)

KAREN: She told you?

ART: I overheard.

KAREN: She said you weren't there—

ART: I wasn't—I'd gone out back to have a smoke.

KAREN: Look, you've gotta understand—that wasn't about you. It was about Connie. The way she pushes and pushes and doesn't listen to anyone else. That's what I meant.

ART: I don't know how you can marry me and still see me as an Invader. I don't. How are you gonna look at our kids?

KAREN: With love. I love you Art.   I do. I don't see you as an Invader. I see you as my husband.

ART: Why? Because I'm a warrior? Because I fucking sucked at that.

KAREN: No. I love you because you're sweet, and you're kind and you love honestly and straight out. You don't play games. You don't waste opportunities. You left here to get yourself a new life. That takes a lot of courage. I think you're amazing.

(Beat)

ART: Connie didn't burn down the Longhouse.

KAREN: Okay. It's just that—

ART: *(Cuts her off)* I say Gary has as much reason to do it as anyone. Upset the families and they'll block the wedding. And it will get Connie shunned. I'd say that's as good a possibility as any.

KAREN: There's no way—he wouldn't.

ART: I'm gonna take it to the Clan Mothers.

KAREN: But he's not guilty—

ART: We don't know Connie is. I know there's more than one side to this.

(ARTHUR SR sighs loudly, and sits up, startling ART and KAREN.)

KAREN: Sorry, Mr Farmer, we didn't see you.

ARTHUR SR: Where's Brewster?

ART: Not sure. He's on our side, though.

ARTHUR SR: There's other options besides Connie and Gary.

ART: You don't think—

KAREN: Oh geez, I didn't even think of that—of course!

ART: Why does it always have to be one of us, Dad?

KAREN: Brewster makes sense! Don't you see? He'd do anything for Connie, you know that!

ART: Gary would do anything to get us off the Rez.

KAREN: Look, I'm not accusing, but just ask him.

ART: If you ask Gary.

ARTHUR SR: Both of you ask them. You've got a right to, you're fighting for your life together.

(There's a quick knock on the door and BREWSTER *strolls in.)*

BREWSTER: Hey, has she made it back yet?

ART: No. Wasn't she with you?

BREWSTER: Banished me as usual. *(He strolls in and flops down on the sofa, next to* ARTHUR SR*)*

ARTHUR SR: Had a rough night last night?

BREWSTER: Oh, no! That bad, isit? Eh, I was feeling a little raw. Had to take the edge off.

KAREN: You see! I told you—

ART: Shh! Wait—

BREWSTER: What did you tell him, Princess? That I drink? No news there.

ART: No. Not that.

BREWSTER: Someone gonna tell me what's going on?

ARTHUR SR: I'm gonna leave you too to talk. Karen, you want to go for a walk with me?

KAREN: Sure. I'd love to.

(KAREN *and* ARTHUR SR *exit.*)

BREWSTER: Okay. That was subtle. Spill it.

ART: You were drinking last night.

BREWSTER: Well, duh. And—

ART: Well, you know how you get when you're drinking—

BREWSTER: Like I am now, you mean?

ART: Um—

BREWSTER: You can't be trying to pin the Longhouse on me—

ART: Dad thought—

BREWSTER: Your Dad thought I would do that?

ART: Not you. But when you're drinking—

BREWSTER: Oh yeah? Because they kicked me out?

ART: Well yea, and—

BREWSTER: Because that was ten years ago.

ART: Well, Connie's upset—

BREWSTER: Connie gets upset. That's not new.

ART: Let's stop pretending, okay?

BREWSTER: What are you talking about?

ART: It's no secret how you feel about Connie. Its makes a lot of sense. Why not you? We all have old scores to settle with the Longhouses and now, with me marrying Karen, and Connie's reaction— Maybe you couldn't protect her for once—

BREWSTER: You know, I ought to be insulted, but this is too fucking funny. What was I going to do, present the smoking match to her as a token of my undying devotion? I can just see me in court! "Officers, I know what a shitty thing I've done, but you must understand! I did it for Love!" Yep. Sounds like me—

ART: I've seen when you get out of control, Brews. It's possible.

BREWSTER: That's my best friend.

ART: You know I had to ask, don't you?

BREWSTER: Maybe. How do I know you didn't do it?

ART: What?!

BREWSTER: You have as good a reason as any of us. You have the same history as Connie.

ART: I'm marrying into the Longhouse. I wouldn't do that if I wasn't over it.

BREWSTER: Bullshit, you're not over it. You're getting married but you're not over it. Maybe this wedding is too much. Maybe it's an easy out for you.

ART: Okay. It's bullshit—I know. I'm just tired of them blaming us for everything.

BREWSTER: Likewise.

(End of scene)

Scene 4

(Lights up on the livingroom. CONNIE and ARTHUR SR eat breakfast.)

ARTHUR SR: Good breakfast.

CONNIE: Thanks. *(She pours him a little more coffee.)*

ARTHUR SR: Delicious coffee, too! You should become a Chef.

CONNIE: Okay. Quit trying to butter me up. I'm fine. They're gonna blame me, but I'm fine.

ARTHUR SR: Yeah. Of course you are. You didn't do it, did you?

CONNIE: What? No, Dad, I didn't! How could you ask me?!

ARTHUR SR: You have a temper on you. Just like your mother. She used to aim it at me all the time. I knew when I saw that glare, to run for a bit.

CONNIE: Not funny, Dad.

ARTHUR SR: No. But I had to ask.

CONNIE: It doesn't matter anyway. They're going to blame me no matter what.

ARTHUR SR: Yeah. Probably.

CONNIE: What am I going to do, Dad?

ARTHUR SR: Maybe it might be time to finally go to the city.

CONNIE: No—not like this—

ARTHUR SR: Think about it! All those opportunities. You could become a Chef! An Indian Chef. Bring real corn soup to the masses.

CONNIE: The masses don't deserve good cornsoup.

(ART *enters with a knock.* KAREN *is close on his heels.* BREWSTER *strolls in behind them, just watching.*)

ART: They're voting to shun you, Connie.

CONNIE: That's quick. Gary's a fast worker.

KAREN: Go and speak to them. Give them a chance, they may listen.

CONNIE: Yeah? Would you?

KAREN: I'm here, aren't I?

CONNIE: I didn't do it.

KAREN: Okay.

CONNIE: I'm serious.

KAREN: I know. Whatever you say—

CONNIE: What if I say that your brother is a rat who was just waiting for a chance to get me.

KAREN: Don't start on Gary, okay? I'm here with Art, supporting Art and my soon-to-be sister, but don't ask me to trash my brother. It's not going to happen.

(A loud pounding on the door. GARY enters. He strides over to KAREN.)

GARY: I saw you come in here. I can't believe it! Get your stuff, we're going.

ARTHUR SR: Gary, I don't think Karen's finished her visit yet.

GARY: I'm sorry sir, but this is a shunned house. She's not supposed to be here.

ARTHUR SR: Am I shunned?

GARY: No sir, but this is Connie's house—

ART: It's a family house.

GARY: Get your stuff, Karen.

KAREN: No! I'm not leaving.

BREWSTER: Doesn't seem like she wants to leave.

GARY: My sister is not marrying into this family!

KAREN: You have no say! I choose my own husband.

ARTHUR SR: Your mother still gives her blessing.

GARY: My mother isn't thinking clearly.

KAREN: Oh! Let me tell her you said that!

GARY: You think this is funny? This witch destroyed your Longhouse! How could you want the brother of a woman like that?

ARTHUR SR: You're out of line, Gary. Coming here like this, and going to the Clan Mothers—that was way out of line.

GARY: You know I'm right, sir. She did it. *(To* CONNIE*)* You're done. You've finally done it. It doesn't matter where you show your face anymore because no one will see it.

BREWSTER: What makes them so sure it's her?

GARY: Who else?

BREWSTER: Could've been an accident.

GARY: Not the way it burned. It was incinerated.

BREWSTER: Some people thought I did it—in a drunken stupor.

GARY: You're an asshole but you're still Ongwehonewe. You'd never—

CONNIE: Still a charmer, huh Gary?

BREWSTER: Then there's always…you.

GARY: Have another drink, why don't you?

BREWSTER: Don't mind if I do? *(He pulls out a flask.)* You first, brother—

KAREN: Gary doesn't drink.

BREWSTER: Did last night.

GARY: *(To* BREWSTER*)* Very funny.

KAREN: What? What are you talking about?

BREWSTER: It's entirely possible that your brother did it, Karen. He was in a mood.

KAREN: He's always in a mood. That means nothing.

GARY: Now I get it! For some reason, I thought you and I were friends again.

BREWSTER: Of course we are Gary, and like any good friend, I'm only doing this for your own good.

KAREN: Gary doesn't drink!

BREWSTER: Only once in a blue moon, but like all folks who don't drink much, it hits him harder, doesn't it Gary?

KAREN: Not my brother. Alcohol is poison for our people. He's always saying that. He would never drink and certainly not with you.

GARY: Karen, get your stuff. You don't need to talk to these people anymore.

KAREN: I'm staying.

GARY: You can't.

KAREN: I told you, I've made my choice. Art will be my husband.

GARY: How can you turn your back on your family?

KAREN: This is my family, too, now.

ART: Brews, did he really drink with you?

BREWSTER: Happened to run into him in that little bar by his work. I like it there. Like the TVs in the johns. Caught our Gary having a beer.

KAREN: I already told you—Gary, tell him to stop lying. *(Beat)* Gary?

BREWSTER: Haven't you ever wondered why his favorite hangout is a bar?

CONNIE: Gary's a good hypocrite. I've always known that.

ART: Alcohol loosens inhibitions.

KAREN: How long have you been doing this?

ARTHUR SR: It's a bit surprising for a Clan Chief.

GARY: Sometimes, I have to—step out of it all, okay? Just one beer, that's all it ever is.

KAREN: I don't know what's worse, finding out you drink, or finding out you lie about it. What other stuff have you been hiding?

BREWSTER: *(To* GARY*)* You had quite a few, as I recall. *(To* KAREN*)* He doesn't approve of the wedding. He really does think Art is marrying you to get into the Longhouse.

ART: Wow. You don't think much of your sister, do you?

GARY: You talk a good game, kid. But you forget, I know where you come from. Connie's been programing you since you could walk.

KAREN: It isn't true.

GARY: I don't want you hurt Karen, that's all. I'm looking out for you.

KAREN: By breaking up my wedding? Nice looking out.

GARY: You have to listen to reason.

KAREN: Does Mom know you drink?

GARY: It's just once in a while—

KAREN: Did you do it?

GARY: What?!

BREWSTER: If you're so honorable, Gary—answer the question.

GARY: This is ridiculous—Don't let them manipulate you! Our family is the Longhouse. I couldn't burn it down.

ARTHUR SR: Actually, it makes sense.

BREWSTER: A burned Longhouse is much easier to handle than a brother in law that you hate.

KAREN: I should've realized. This is my fault. I knew you were upset about the wedding. I should've talked to you more—explained...

ART: I think its my turn to go to the Clan Mothers.

GARY: Amazing! This is—you're manipulating everything.

CONNIE: Yeah, welcome to my world.

GARY: Don't listen to them, Karen! They're good at this! Getting sympathies and twisting situations!

KAREN: Go away. Please. Just leave me alone.

GARY: *(To* CONNIE*)* Congratulations! You've exceeded all my expectations! *(He exits.)*

KAREN: Connie, I'm sorry. I'm so ashamed.

ART: I'm going to go speak to the Clan Mothers. We'll get you back in! Won't we Art?

(They dash off. CONNIE *runs to* BREWSTER *and gives him a big hug.)*

CONNIE: Thank you!

BREWSTER: All in a day's work.

CONNIE: If you're around later, I might be by the river.

BREWSTER: Oh yeah?

*(*BREWSTER *turns to leave, bowing formally before he departs.* CONNIE *watches him go with a smile.)*

*(*ARTHUR SR *clears the plates.)*

CONNIE: Don't clean up, Dad, I'll do it.

ARTHUR SR: It's no problem. Brewster should be a lawyer. Getting Gary to admit all in front of Karen.

CONNIE: Amazing that they went drinking together.

ARTHUR SR: Yep got him drunk, too. Kind of strange, ain't it?

CONNIE: How?

ARTHUR SR: So out of character for him.

CONNIE: What are you trying to say?

ARTHUR SR: Wonder how Brewster persuaded Gary to have a drink?

CONNIE: Wait a minute, Dad—I didn't make Gary drink! I didn't make him hang out with Brewster.

ARTHUR SR: True, he wasn't innocent. *(Stacks the dishes to take to the kitchen)* You might want to think about the city. It's a great place for a young woman with ambition.

(End of scene)

Scene 5

(The riverbank. CONNIE is playing "with" FLINT and smoking. After a beat, BREWSTER enters. He's changed his shirt and combed his hair.)

CONNIE: Took you long enough! Wow! Shirt change. You look good.

BREWSTER: Thank you Ma'am. I figured since it was an occasion, maybe we could go to town.

CONNIE: Well, well, Brewster White. Are you asking me on a date?

BREWSTER: I just thought we should celebrate. You know? Gary finally getting what he deserves.

CONNIE: You were brilliant. Dad said you could've been a lawyer.

BREWSTER: I just thought things should go our way for once. *(Beat)* You're home free now!

CONNIE: Pardon?

BREWSTER: You're in the clear. You have nothing to worry about.

CONNIE: Wait a minute, what are you saying?

BREWSTER: There's only one thing I need. We never discuss it. I don't want to think too much about it.

CONNIE: You think I did it.

BREWSTER: Oh come on, Con. But it's okay I know how much they've hurt you, it's okay.

CONNIE: That's big of you.

BREWSTER: I just wanna forget this whole thing.

(Beat)

CONNIE: You'd like that wouldn't you? That's your favorite thing.

BREWSTER: What?

CONNIE: That's why you like your whiskey. You like to pretend that things aren't happening. You like to numb yourself into a big nothing.

BREWSTER: Yeah? Maybe. A drink makes it a lot easier to take you, sweetheart. You and your temper. Your selfishness.

CONNIE: Selfish?

BREWSTER: Yeah, hon. Selfish. What do you call trying to break up Art's wedding? What do you call burning down people's spiritual home? Just because they won't let you in? Selfish. And, crazy rage. Outta do something about that. *(He pulls out his flask and takes a sip.)*

CONNIE: Yeah? Well, at least rage has a focus. You float around the Rez in a haze, pretending that you're above it all. Nothing touches you. Nothing hurts you.

BREWSTER: Why does that bother you? Do you want to hurt me Connie?

CONNIE: How can I hurt somebody who's not even there most of the time?

BREWSTER: I've always been there for you. I've done everything I can to help you. I just saved your ass and got a little revenge.
What else could you possibly want? Because this is about it.

CONNIE: I will find a place here.

BREWSTER: You have a place here. It's just not the one you want.

CONNIE: It's so easy for you. You had everything and you threw it all away!

(Beat)

BREWSTER: If you're thinking I should dry out and rejoin the Longhouse—you're dreaming. Not gonna happen and it wouldn't affect you even if I did.

CONNIE: No. I guess not. So? We done here?

BREWSTER: Yeah. I am. Finally. *(He exits.)*

CONNIE: *(To herself)* I WILL—I will find my place here. *(Suddenly chilly, she hugs herself.)*

(The WOMAN *enters, pulling* FLINT *by the ear. She finally has the buckskin bag back. She spots* CONNIE *standing alone and she reaches forward to give her the small bag of tobacco.* FLINT *tries to grab it, the* WOMAN *grabs his ear again.)*

WOMAN: Flint wants to apologize. Don't you?

*(*FLINT *shakes his head. The* WOMAN *gives him a glare.)*

WOMAN: He didn't mean any harm at all.

(The WOMAN *pokes* FLINT *and he nods his head yes.)*

WOMAN: It's not his fault! It's just the darkness—his realm. It just begs for a little bit of trouble-making.

(The WOMAN *smiles at the audience, and she leads* FLINT *offstage. Lights down on* CONNIE *standing alone.)*

(Blackout)

END OF PLAY

www.ingramcontent.com/pod-product-compliance
Lightning Source LLC
Chambersburg PA
CBHW052211090426
42741CB00010B/2502